INTRODUCTION

TO

TRUE LOVE WAITS®

by Jimmy Hester

LifeWay Press®
Nashville, Tennessee

ISBN: 0-6331-9532-4

Dewey Decimal Classification Number: 306.73
Subject Heading: TRUE LOVE WAITS \ SEXUAL ABSTINENCE

Printed in the United States of America

Student Ministry Publishing
LifeWay Church Resources
One LifeWay Plaza
Nashville, Tennessee 37234-0174

We believe the Bible has God for its author; salvation for its
end; and truth, without any mixture of error, for its matter and
that all Scripture is totally true and trustworthy. The 2000
statement of *The Baptist Faith and Message*
is our doctrinal guideline.

CONTENTS

WRITER:
JIMMY HESTER

One day back in 1993, Jimmy Hester and Richard Ross were sitting around a table in the cafeteria at work. They were talking about the cry they were hearing from teenagers (and parents of teens) to express their beliefs about sexual abstinence until marriage. Jimmy and Richard took a napkin and sketched the plan for what became True Love Waits. Since then, Jimmy and his wife, Kim, have experienced the teenage years with their two sons, Jordan and Justin. Both young men have made a commitment to True Love Waits.

Today, Jimmy is Senior Director of Student Ministry Publishing at LifeWay Christian Resources and the coordinator of the True Love Waits Team. His component publishes resources for students (seventh grade through college), their leaders, and their families through print, multimedia, and electronic formats.

INTRODUCING TRUE LOVE WAITS

WELCOME! I'M GLAD YOU DECIDED to open this booklet and learn about True Love Waits. You see and hear messages all around you every day about sex. It's not just in health class at school; it is in movies, on billboards, and in conversations with your friends. True Love Waits is another message about sex, but I think you will see it as a completely different kind of message. True Love Waits is a message from the creator of sex—God!

My hope is that these pages will inform and inspire you. At the conclusion of your walk through this book, I hope you will make or confirm your commitment to live a life of purity, including remaining sexually abstinent until marriage.

This book addresses questions many students have asked about True Love Waits and sexual purity. The answers to the questions are compiled from several sources. Since True Love Waits began in 1993, much has been said and written to teach and encourage—and it's all good stuff! What you find in the following discussion is the best of the best based on the messages from wise counselors like Susan Lanford, Ann Cannon, Paul Kelly, Bill Hughes, Kristi Cherry, Paul Turner, Matt Tullos, Jay and Diane Strack, David Payne, Tony Rankin, Richard Ross, and others.

Not only will it be beneficial to read through the entire booklet, but we believe it can serve as a great resource in the days ahead when you have questions or when you are asked questions by your friends. You may have the chance to study through this booklet with others at your church or at school. In fact, you may want to lead some friends through a study of this booklet. To help with that, we have placed some suggestions for teaching online at www.truelovewaits.com.

True Love Waits addresses a huge spiritual issue in your life. I hope that God will speak to you as you read and study. So read carefully and prayerfully.

WHAT IS SEXUAL PURITY?

TRUE LOVE WAITS is a call to sexual purity. Students all over the world have responded to this call, committing to lifestyles of purity. It is a message clearly taught in the Bible. Your decision about sexual purity can make all the difference in your dating relationships, in your family, and in your future marriage. Sexual purity is a big deal. So, let's get to the questions.

What exactly is sexual purity?

People have defined sexual purity in different ways, so I want to be really clear about what I mean by sexual purity. Sexual purity includes abstaining from sexual intercourse until marriage, but that is not all it means. Jesus' definition goes far beyond sexual abstinence.

> Jesus said, "You have heard that it was said, 'You shall not commit adultery.' But I tell you, everyone who looks at a woman to lust for her has already committed adultery with her in his heart" (Matt. 5:27-28).

Which of these do you think is part of sexual purity for unmarried persons.

☐ saying no to sexual intercourse, oral sex, and even sexual touching
☐ saying no to a physical relationship that causes you to be "turned on" sexually
☐ not dwelling on thoughts of sex
☐ not looking at pornography or pictures or reading books that feed sexual thoughts

I hope you marked all four answers; all of them can be parts of sexual purity. Sexual purity does include sexual abstinence before marriage, but it is more than setting limits on your behavior. Sexual purity

8

is a total commitment of your sexual needs, desires, thoughts, and actions to God.

Some people say, "I'll be sexually pure until I get married." Don't miss this: Sexual purity does not end with marriage. Marriage partners are supposed to experience sexual love with each other. For a married person, purity means being completely faithful to his or her spouse in both thought and deed. (See Heb. 13:4.)

Worth a Thought:
How does your life measure up to Jesus' standard for sexual purity? Do you need to make any changes?

Is sexual purity really in the Bible?

Absolutely! You will see biblical references throughout this booklet as we address issues related to sexual purity because sexual morality is an important part of the Bible's teachings. Both the Old and New Testaments call people to lives of sexual purity. From Sodom and Gomorrah in Genesis 19 to Jesus' message to the churches in Revelation 2, the Bible calls people to lives of purity.

Let me give you an example. When the church first began, almost all believers were Jews who trusted Christ for salvation. Then Gentiles began to trust

Christ for salvation. There was much disagreement among Jewish Christians. Some believed a Gentile would have to follow the Jewish laws and traditions in order to be a Christian. Others believed that most Jewish traditions were not important for Gentiles. The leaders of the early church gathered to pray and listen for God's leadership. The response the church leaders sent to the Gentile converts included the instructions found in Acts 15:29. Sexual purity was one of the few things the early church insisted on for every Christian.

> **That you abstain from food offered to idols, from blood, from eating anything that has been strangled, and from sexual immorality. If you keep yourselves from these things, you will do well (Acts 15:29).**

Some say that the Bible doesn't speak to many issues related to sexuality. They reason that if the Bible doesn't specifically address a certain issue, it must be OK. You may be surprised at how much the Bible does specifically address. The Bible completely prohibits some sexual actions such as homosexuality (see Rom. 1:26-28), sexual acts with animals (see Ex. 22:19), and prostitution (see 1 Cor. 6:16-17). Beyond that, the Bible also provides clear principles that apply to any sexual activity. These biblical principles are true for all people in all cultures at any time.

1. The Bible declares that sex is good and was designed by God. (See Gen. 1:28.)
2. The Bible requires sexual abstinence prior to marriage. (See 1 Cor. 6:18.)
3. The Bible views sexual intercourse as a bonding of two persons that should occur only in marriage. (See Gen. 2:24.)
4. The Bible insists that the sexual relationship in marriage exist in an exclusive and faithful commitment of one man and one woman. (See Heb. 13:4.)
5. The Bible condemns sexual relations other than relations between one man and one woman. (See Eph. 5:3.)

Worth Discussing:
Do all of these principles make sense? Which of these principles is the most difficult for you?

Why did God create sexual beings?

God created people as male and female. He gave the man and woman the ability to enjoy an intimate relationship with each other. In fact, God designed the relationship between a man and a woman to be the ultimate human relationship. Only their relationship with Him would be more significant. In His design, sexual oneness would bring them together in unity and allow them to bear and raise children.

God's plan for sex should be cherished as part of God's original design.

God designed sexuality as something wonderful, something good, something holy. Using sex in a way that defies God's standard causes something good to be used for evil. Disobeying God leads to emptiness and pain.

God created you to be a sexual being. His intention for you is that you experience the full joy of His gift of sex, but only within the context in which He designed it: a committed marriage relationship. You can experience God's very best for you, but to do that you will have to live purely. In order to live a pure life you will have to guard your body, emotions, and mind from sexual temptations.

How do you "guard your body"?

God designed physical, sexual love to knit two lives together. Jesus explained God's plan.

> "Haven't you read," He replied, "that He who created them in the beginning 'made them male and female,' and He also said: 'For this reason a man will leave his father and mother and be joined to his wife, and the two will become one flesh?' So they are no longer two, but one flesh. Therefore what God has joined

**together, man must not separate"
(Matt. 19:4-6).**

God created physical love to bind a man and a woman together for life. When unmarried men and women get physical with each other, their bodies react no differently than the married person's body. Their bodies want to have intercourse because it is the way they are made.

Sexual purity means unmarried men and women must guard their bodies. Our bodies are to be sanctified for God's use. *Sanctification* is the lifelong process of becoming like Jesus. Only as we become like Jesus will we be able to control and guard our bodies (vessels).

> **For this is God's will, your sanctification: that you abstain from sexual immorality, so that each of you knows how to possess his own vessel in sanctification and honor, not with lustful desires, like the Gentiles who don't know God (1 Thess. 4:3-5).**

How do you "guard your emotions"?

Most teenagers experience a flood of feelings. Feelings can make it difficult to sort out true love from attraction. Many teenagers want to know whether or not they have found true love in a dating relationship. True love that occurs between a man and a woman includes several elements: a deep, long-lasting friendship; love that is given even when it is undeserved; and physical attraction that leads to erotic love.

There are two ways people "fall in love." One is that they give the passionate love they should have for God to each other instead. The other is that they passionately love God and He draws them together. Out of their mutual love for God, a passionate love for each other grows.

Love is not the same as sex. Sexual arousal is not the same as love. The Bible describes real love as more meaningful and more enduring.

Love is patient; love is kind. Love does not envy; is not boastful; is not conceited; does not act improperly; is not selfish; is not provoked; does not keep a record of wrongs; finds no joy in unrighteousness, but rejoices in the truth; bears all things, believes all things, hopes all things, endures all things (1 Cor. 13:4-7).

True love is so much more than a emotion. It is an action and a commitment. True love loves even when it doesn't feel like loving.

How do you "guard your mind"?

Computer geeks have a saying, "Garbage in, garbage out." That means whatever you get out of a computer is directly related to what you put into a computer.

The same is true with your mind. Your mind has the ability to store and recall vast amounts of information and images. The images you see, the messages you hear, and the moments you experience are fed into and captured in your mind. If those things you receive are good and healthy, then your mind will be filled with good and healthy thoughts and images. If not, "garbage in, garbage out."

In the culture in which you live, you will be bombarded by a flood of images. You can't drive down the street without seeing billboards plastered with sexual images trying to sell almost any product. Guarding your mind means being careful about what messages you dwell on. You may not be able to tear every billboard down, but you can divert your eyes and look away. You can't change what they air on television, but you can choose the shows you watch. You can't change what is said over the radio, but you can change the station. The Apostle Paul had it right. Read what he said to the Philippian Christians.

Finally brothers, whatever is true, whatever is honorable, whatever is just, whatever is pure, whatever is lovely, whatever is commendable—if there is any moral excellence and if there is any praise—dwell on these things. Do what you have learned and received and heard and seen in me, and the God of peace will be with you (Phil. 4:8-9).

Worth Discussing:
Which is hardest: guarding your body, your emotions, or your mind?

SEXUAL PURITY EXPERIENCED

YOU MAY BE SAYING, "I can see that the Bible teaches sexual purity, but is this for real? How can a teenager really control his or her sexual appetites and live the way you describe?" I'm glad you asked.

How can I fight temptation?

You are in a lifelong fight to live a victorious Christian life. It is a fight you can win because of Christ's victory in your life. Paul told Timothy to "Fight the good fight for the faith"(1 Tim. 6:12).

However, the Bible never says to fight temptation. We are told to flee temptation, not to fight it. In both letters to Timothy, Paul said to "run from these things" (1 Tim. 6:11), and "flee from youthful passions" (2 Tim. 2:22). Paul also told the Christians in Corinth to "Flee from sexual immorality!" (1 Cor. 6:18). Staying sexually pure depends on a consistent response to sexual temptation—and that is to get away from it as quickly as possible.

Worth a Thought:
Have you been fighting temptation or fleeing it?

How do I guard my body, emotions, and mind?

Now we get to the practical stuff. Spend a moment and reflect on your life in these three areas.

Body: How far is too far?
For some couples, brief kissing will be fine. For many couples, anything more than holding hands

will be too much. And unless you are dead, the heavy, make-out type of kissing is across the boundary because it makes your body want to go to the next level. You can control your body. God gave you a brain as an important part of your body. Learn how to use your brain and your body responsibly.

Emotions: How do I handle my feelings?
Do you say, "I love you," when you really mean, "I think you are fun to be with"? Do you hang out with many friends or are you always just around the person you date? How do you spend your time together? Do you talk about, "If we were married…"? You can control the depth of your emotions by monitoring and adjusting your involvement with others.

Mind: How do I keep my thoughts pure?
When you talk to a member of the opposite sex, do you look at her eyes, or her body? When you find yourself tempted to think impure thoughts about an attractive member of the opposite sex, what do you do? Have you ever considered thanking God for creating attractive guys/girls and asking Him to help you to be patient to wait for the one He has for you? What's in your room at home? Do you need to remove things that would lead you to think lustful thoughts? Have you made a commitment not to view pornography? Are you careful with the stories and articles you read? What movies and television shows do you watch? Do you avoid spending a lot

19

of time with people who dwell on sexual conversation or sexual jokes? You can control your mind by making sure you feed it a healthy diet of pure thoughts.

Worth a Thought:
What is one thing you should change in each area?

Is sex a bad thing?

Absolutely not! God designed us as sexual beings. He invented sex! He also made a place for it—marriage.

> This is why a man leaves his father and mother and bonds with his wife, and they become one flesh (Gen. 2:24).

The sexual relationship allows the two to become one flesh. The Bible speaks of sexual immorality, so there must also be such a thing as sexual morality, right? That morality is based on God's plan for sex.

What are the dangers of having sex before marriage?

Without going into a lot of detail, the list of reasons range from things that affect your relationship with God to the effects on earthly relationships.

20

- Distant relationship with God
- Feelings of guilt and shame
- Picking up a sexually transmitted disease
- Contracting HIV and AIDS which leads to death
- Experiencing an unwanted pregnancy
- Loss of self-respect and the respect of others
- Strained relationships with family and friends
- Psychological and emotional damage
- Ineffective witness for Jesus Christ

What if things just happen?

Sex is not an accident. Sex is progressive; one act leads to another. Things won't "just happen" if you set boundaries and stick to them. If you make the decision now to abstain from sex, then you will already know the answer before you encounter any compromising situation. Plus, the Holy Spirit gives you self-control to use when you are tempted.

Where do I draw the line?

Purity is the plumb line for making decisions about sexual attitudes and actions. A Christian view of sexuality does not ask, "How far from purity can I wander before I have sinned?" A Christian view of purity guides us to turn toward purity and seek it in our attitude and actions.

Josh McDowell explains,

> **When one person's desires begin to rise above
> what is right and spiritually healthy for the
> other person, they've crossed the 'line.'[1]**

McDowell provides a simple diagram to illustrate
where the "line" is for most people. Although all
sexual acts are not included in the diagram, you can
easily place others where they should go in the pro-
gression from abstinence to sexual intercourse.

> **Abstinence**
> **Holding Hands**
> **Hugging**
> **Casual Kissing**
> _____
> **Prolonged Kissing**
> **Light Petting**
> **Heavy Petting**
> **Intercourse**

**I don't believe most healthy Christians in a
dating relationship, whatever their age, can
progress much beyond this line without asking for trouble. You need to realize that past
this point you begin to arouse in each other
desires that cannot be righteously fulfilled
outside of marriage.[2]**

Is it wrong to express affection or flirt?

Behavior needs to be appropriate for the occasion. At school, church, or youth group activities, displays of affection are inappropriate. Inappropriate public displays of affection anywhere can embarrass others and make the couple look silly.

Flirting can be harmful when it teases another person by explicit or implied sexual advances. Harmful flirting can include revealing clothing, bumping into another person, sexual gestures, or suggestive talk. Light flirting such as writing notes, winking, smiling, and talking on the phone is fine. This innocent flirting actually can help you learn to communicate with the opposite sex.

Why do I need dating guidelines?

Compare relationships to a sport, such as volleyball or football. What would the game be like without boundary lines? The same is true in dating. Without boundaries, someone will likely get hurt physically and/or emotionally. It is always good to have someone around (like the referee) to hold each of you accountable to the rules.

Your parents can be a helpful part of your dating experiences, if you will let them. Talk with them about developing a dating contract. Work together to set up a few guidelines that protect you and make everyone happy. Write them down and review them often. Include guidelines like these:

- Age when you start going out with a group
- Age when you start single dating
- Reasons to date
- Places you should be allowed to go
- The type of people you want to date (age, interests, spiritual condition)
- Which nights you can go out and the curfews
- Cost and how to pay for the date

These guidelines will provide you and your parents common ground of understanding. They will also give you something to fall back on when you have to make a tough dating decision.

Isn't everybody doing it?

Everyone is not doing it! Research studies conducted by many universities and government agencies indicate that a majority of teenagers are abstaining from sex. If you hang around people who are sexually active, however, the peer pressure to have sex increases significantly.

Am I still pure if I was a victim of rape?

Becoming sexually impure is a matter of sin. When you choose to act in a way that you know goes

against God's standards, you sin and become impure. Rape is an awful crime of violence. A victim of
rape did not choose to have sex, and therefore did
not commit a sexual sin. That person has not com-
promised personal purity.

If you have been the victim of rape, you need to
seek help. A rapist counts on his victims to hide his
crime out of a sense of undue shame. Tell an adult
you can trust immediately. Realize that God loves
you incredibly and will continue to love you as you
heal from this terrible experience.

What if I've had sex before marriage?

There is not enough room here to completely deal
with that question. You need to pick up a copy of
When True Love Doesn't Wait (ISBN 0-7673-9076-
8). Here's one word of encouragement from that
booklet:

**If you consented to the sexual acts, then you
can receive a second virginity. Although there
may be no way to replace the physical virginity, an emotional virginity is even more precious and important to have when you marry.
Having sex is easy. Deciding not to is difficult.
Choosing not to have sex at this point says a
great deal about your commitment to future
relationships. Choosing to remain pure until**

25

you marry is the most incredible thing you can do.[3]

Sin does have consequences; you may be dealing with those now as a result of sexual sin. The good news is that there are people around you who can walk with you through tough times. Don't be afraid to talk with a counselor, minister, or parent for help.

Whatever your sin, God offers second chances! His forgiveness is a gift. We don't deserve it, but He offers it to us anyway! That's called grace!

1. Josh McDowell, "So you wonder How Far?" *True Love Waits Bible,* (Nashville: Broadman and Holman Publishers, 1996), 1104.
2. Ibid, 1105.
3. D. Tony Rankin and Richard Ross, *When True Love Doesn't Wait* (Nashville: LifeWay Press, 1998).

What Is TRUE LOVE WAITS?

SEXUAL PURITY IS the call of God for every Christian. How can you live a pure life? Hundreds of thousands of students all over the world have decided to commit themselves to sexual purity by signing a True Love Waits pledge. That commitment is making a tremendous difference in their lives and in the cultures in which they live.

What is True Love Waits?

True Love Waits is an international campaign challenging and empowering students to make a commitment to sexual purity, live it everyday, and proclaim it to others. God has called you to live a life of sexual purity. True Love Waits is all about following God's plan for purity.

Most students discover True Love Waits through their church or a student organization. Many churches hold studies, worship services, and special events focused on purity. Regardless how you get involved, the challenge of True Love Waits is to sign a commitment card that states your pledge to a life of purity, which includes sexual abstinence until you get married.

True Love Waits began in 1993. Many Christian teenagers were trying to live according to God's commands, but the loudest voices seemed to say that all teens were involved in sex. True Love Waits was born out of a cry from teenagers and their parents to express their conviction about the importance of sexual abstinence until marriage.

Since then, hundreds of thousands of students all over the world have signed True Love Waits commitment cards and displayed them in public places to indicate their stand for purity. Religious denominations, student organizations, health agencies, Christian entertainers and authors, and other groups have joined the sexual abstinence movement. True Love Waits has been featured in magazines and newspapers, on all the major television networks, and on radio programs around the world.

Regardless of what you have done in the past, you can start living a sexually pure life now by joining the host of students who have already signed the True Love Waits pledge.

Worth a Thought:
How could you take a stand for sexual purity in your church and town? What could you do that might make a difference for other students?

What is the True Love Waits pledge?

The True Love Waits pledge is simple and yet profoundly meaningful:

Believing that true love waits, I make a commitment to God, myself, my family, my friends, my future mate, and my future children to a lifetime of purity including sexual abstinence from this day until the day I enter a biblical marriage relationship.

29

It is a promise to be sexually pure. It was developed to help students join with others around the world in taking a stand. Each phrase was written to encourage students taking the pledge to have a sense of accountability to others. The next few questions will explore the True Love Waits pledge in detail.

Why make a commitment to God?

"The reason I am waiting to have sex until I am married is that my Lord commanded it and I will obey. God loves me and wants the best for me." —Monique

True love starts with love for God. Jesus made that clear. Making a commitment to God acknowledges His proper place in your life.

" 'You shall love the Lord your God with all your heart, with all your soul, and with all your mind.' This is the greatest and most important commandment" (Matt. 22:37-38).

Worth a Thought:
Have you made the decision to place your life in the hands of Christ?
If not, see page 46.

Why make a commitment to myself?

"In my middle teens I had some issues with church, school, my girlfriend—just about everything seemed wrong. I took my eyes off God and did things my way. The worst decision I made was breaking my commitment to abstinence. The guilt haunted me. When I met my future wife, I felt I didn't deserve her. It has taken a long time to ask God for forgiveness. I can almost forgive myself." —Doug

Living a sexually permissive life hurts other people in your life, but it also ends up hurting you. (See Prov. 6:25-29.) Making a commitment to yourself means that you intend to keep your life pure so that you can experience God's best.

Why make a commitment to my family?

If you truly love the members of your family, you won't act irresponsibly related to sex (and many other things). An irresponsible life can destroy relationships. Responsibility calls for being honest, following family agreements and rules, and living up to commitments. Making a commitment to your family to live a life of purity is a responsible act that encourages healthy family relationships.

Worth Discussing:
What does your family expect of you? How do you feel about the responsibility you show your family?

Why make a commitment to my friends?

When you agree to stand arm-in-arm with your friends in a commitment to sexual purity, you can avoid a variety of problems. Physical problems include sexually transmitted diseases and unwanted pregnancies. Emotional problems include guilt and insecurity. Social problems include broken relationships and mistrust. When you make a commitment to your friends, you are telling them that you will work together with them so that both you and they make good decisions about your romantic feelings. They can trust you to do the right thing. That makes you a true friend.

Worth Discussing:
How can friendship help as you seek to please God in the area of sexuality? How can it help in other areas of your life?

Why commit to my future mate?

"True Love Waits was an easy decision when I was 15 and not dating. I had moments of temptation, but the Holy Spirit kept me pure until my wedding night. After getting married, I know it was worth the wait. Now we have an incredible foundation on which to build the rest of our lives." —Jessica

Sexual activity before marriage gives away something precious. A person can certainly be forgiven for past sexual mistakes. However, making a commitment to your future mate now is a promise to save for him or her that precious part of you that can only be given away for the first time to one person.

> Marriage must be respected by all, and the marriage bed kept undefiled, because God will judge immoral people and adulterers (Heb. 13:4).

Worth Discussing:
How do you imagine your future husband or wife? How would you feel if you knew he or she is waiting for you sexually even before knowing you?

Why commit to my future children?

> Sons are indeed a heritage from the Lord, children, a reward (Psalm 127:3).

Children are gifts from God. You may never have children, but if you do, those gifts deserve to enter

33

this world in the best of circumstances—free from disease, into a healthy family, and welcomed by everyone. Early sexual involvement could mean having a child before you are ready. It could even mean creating health problems because of diseases you obtain long before having children. Making a commitment to your future children indicates your concern for their well-being.

What is a biblical marriage relationship?

Today many people are confused about marriage. Some insist that any two people living together in a so-called meaningful relationship, no matter what sex they may be, form a kind of marriage. That is not God's definition of marriage.

The Bible presents a clear picture of marriage: one man and one woman uniting to share life and be faithful to each other for their lifetime. God created marriage for companionship, sexual relations, and the raising of children. Christians should model godly and healthy marriages for a mixed-up world.

Is True Love Waits about more than not having sex?

True Love Waits is about following God's plan for sexual purity. Purity includes refraining from sexual intercourse before marriage, but that is not all.

A pure life involves building healthy relationships with God, friends, family, boyfriends or girlfriends, and even your future mate and children. A pure life is free from guilt. It allows an open line of communication with the God of the universe. God requires purity not because He wants to place a difficult task on you. He requires purity because it will allow you to live a full and meaningful life.

Worth Discussing:
What are the biggest obstacles for teenagers to live sexually pure lives? How can you overcome those?

TRUE LOVE WAITS EXPERIENCED

"Because I have decided it is not an option for me to have sex before I get married, I will never have to worry about a STD. I'll never have to worry that I've gotten someone pregnant. There is incredible freedom in that." —Sam

Why take the True Love Waits pledge?

PEOPLE ARE CAPABLE OF dreaming up all kinds of corrupt ways of expressing human sexuality. We see this in detail on television, movies, and videos. After viewing such corruption for a while, many people even begin to believe that it is normal to express their sexuality in ways that are totally contrary to God's design of sex. There was a time when our society discouraged people from such acts, but those values seem to have broken down today. The results are terrible. Our world needs guidelines that will encourage healthy understanding and practice of sexuality.

The casual attitude toward sexual issues that so many people seem to have produces mistrust, emptiness, disillusionment, and ultimately, shattered relationships. God has given us teachings in the Bible to guide us in making wise decisions. God's principles protect us from the consequences of sexual sin. They also are commands that require our obedience.

What are the personal benefits of delaying sex until marriage?

There are many reasons for saving sex for marriage. The Bible makes it clear that living a sexually pure life is required in order to obey Christ. However, a number of people in our culture are beginning to see the benefits to sexual purity.

Let's look at the results of a recent survey called "SexSmarts." "SexSmarts" is an ongoing information partnership between the Kaiser Family Foundation and *seventeen* magazine to provide young people with information on sexual health issues. Consider this paragraph from their report.

> **Teens agree that delaying sex has a variety of personal benefits, ranging from respect to personal control. More than nine in 10 note that abstaining from sexual activity in high school results in having respect for yourself and enjoying the respect of your family. Waiting also leads teens to feel like they are in control of their relationships, and are behaving consistently with their moral or religious beliefs. Lower on the list, but still significant, is respect from friends. General worry or concern about sexual health risks were also considerable.[1]**

Worth Discussing:
As you look through the reasons many teens gave in the "SexSmarts" study for abstaining from sex, which reasons are most convincing to you?

How do I make a True Love Waits commitment?

First, identify and understand the commitment. Hopefully, the previous section gave you the information and motivation to make a commitment. You might want to review pages 27-35 to make sure you understand the True Love Waits commitment.

Second, privately affirm the commitment in your spirit. Spend time alone with God. Allow His Holy Spirit to be your encourager in making this decision. God's Holy Spirit stands beside you. The Holy Spirit will guide you into all truth and help you in your weakness. Also, acknowledge God's gift of sexuality and thank Him for providing this wonderful part of life.

Third, sign a True Love Waits commitment card. You may be a part of a church that is planning a True Love Waits emphasis. It is great to join other students in signing a card. However, you don't have to wait for your church group. There is a commitment card on page 48 in this booklet. You can sign it right now.

Finally, make your commitment public. You may be wondering, *Do I have to make a public commitment?* This question is important enough that we have devoted an entire section to it. Read on.

39

How important is it that I make a public commitment to sexual purity?

A public commitment has been a positive action for most of the people who have participated in True Love Waits. Church services, banquets, student assemblies, commitment card displays, organizational meetings, and rallies have provided great opportunities for public commitments. Some commitment times are led by adults and include participation from the whole church. Others simply involve students standing before a group and making their commitment known.

While not all students are comfortable doing so, a public commitment gives a strong sense of accountability to many. If you tell others that you pledge to live a pure life, that gives you one more reason to stick to the commitment.

A public commitment to sexual purity is not about shame or guilt. No person should make a commitment to sexual purity just because their friends are making the commitment. No one should make a public commitment because they are afraid of what people will think if they don't. A public commitment to sexual purity should begin with a deep, personal commitment to follow God's plan for sex.

Worth a Thought:
Does the idea of a public commitment to sexual purity scare you? If so, why?

How do I keep my commitment?

The truth is you can't … if you are trying to do it on your own. If you approach a commitment to purity by saying, "I'm going to try to live a pure life," you are probably going to fail. When it is convenient to live purely, you will. When it gets tough, you will crumble. Those who live consistently pure lives have made a commitment to gut it out, no matter how tough it gets. They determine to keep going regardless of how they feel. However, people get in trouble when they make a commitment trusting in their own power to carry it out. You will need God's power to remain sexually pure.

The Bible clearly states that the world will not understand the things of the Spirit. As a result, Christ warned His disciples that because the world hated Him, the world would hate them also. Students who find themselves under attack because they have made a public commitment to purity need to be surrounded and encouraged. Taking a stand of any kind that runs counter to the culture will require strong conviction and perseverance. A commitment to purity will require no less in today's culture.

41

How can I explain to my boyfriend/ girlfriend that I want to wait until I'm married to have sex?

Sharing your personal convictions in your relationships opens up communication and trust. Just be honest about your beliefs and ask about his or hers. When you tell your boyfriend/girlfriend that you want to wait until marriage, you will be able to tell a lot by his or her reaction. If he or she does not agree with or honor your values, then you will need to evaluate the relationship. Common values and beliefs are important in a healthy relationship.

"Hi! My name is Melinda, and I just turned 18 years old. My church did True Love Waits about five years ago. I signed the card basically because it sounded like a good idea, and I hadn't started dating yet. When the rings came out, I decided to get one because it was a good reminder to me of the commitment I had made. Also, I thought it would be neat that I could give it to my husband on my wedding night. I've worn it every day since. I got a boyfriend about a year ago, and because I had already made the commitment and I have the ring as a reminder, it has kept us out of trouble. I never knew that abstaining from pre-marital sex would be so hard, but it is, and I'm glad that I did this program. Without it, I don't think I would have thought about the temptation or why it was wrong. I might have gone ahead and done it. But thanks to the program, I am still a virgin and I plan to be that way until I marry." —Melinda

Worth Discussing:
How strong is a dating relationship if the person you are dating does not honor your commitment to sexual purity?

What can I be doing now, other than just abstaining, that will help me to have a better sexual relationship when I get married?

One great thing you can start doing now is praying for your future spouse. Ask God to protect him or her and keep that person pure. Pray that he or she seeks God and His will. Spend this time of your life getting to know God and letting Him mold you into the person He wants you to be. Strive to keep your mind and body pure.

What can I do to promote True Love Waits?

That's a good question to wrap up this discussion. Here are a couple of thoughts.

1. Model through your attitudes and behavior what it means to live a pure life. Be sensitive to the things you do and say in front of your friends. If you do your best to live a life of purity, God will use your example to work in the lives of others.

2. Take advantage of appropriate opportunities to tell others about the commitment you have made and why you made it. You may be just the person who can guide a friend during a time when he or she is making a decision about being sexually active. Pass this booklet to a friend, or if you don't want to part with your copy, get them a copy of their own. Encourage others to make a True Love Waits commitment and sign a pledge card.

3. Join with others who have made a commitment to sexual abstinence and take a public stand. It may be through your church youth group, or a Christian student organization at school, or through some other group. True Love Waits has become a popular focus during the month of February each year. Seek opportunities to join in the greater sexual abstinence movement and make a difference in our world.

4. Proclaim your belief in and commitment to True Love Waits by wearing a pin, ring, shirt, cap, or some other visual expression. Once your friends see that your commitment is real, they will feel

comfortable coming to you with questions. This will also save you from some awkward situations because they know where you stand.

A final word of encouragement

God wants the best for you. Even though the pressures of this world may seem overwhelming some days, know that God is with you as your encourager and counselor. And He has placed people in this world who serve as His instruments in expressing His love for you. As you make a commitment to sexual abstinence until marriage, remember that you are not alone. Teenagers around the world are choosing sexual purity, and together, your generation can make a difference. God bless you.

1. *Virginity and the First Time,* "SexSmarts," International Communications Research for the Kaiser Family Foundation and *seventeen* magazine, October 2003.

How to Become a Christian

If you have never made a profession of faith in Christ, here is what you need to do.

Admit – Confess to God that you are a sinner. Repent, turning away from your sin.
Romans 3:23; Romans 6:23; Acts 3:19.

Believe – Place your faith in Jesus as God's Son and accept Jesus' gift of forgiveness from sin.
Romans 5:8; Acts 4:12; John 3:16; John 14:6.

Commit – Give your life to Jesus. Ask Him to be your Savior and Lord.
Romans 10:9-10; Romans 10:13; Luke 9:23.

A Simple Prayer – "Lord Jesus, I know I am a sinner and have displeased You in many ways. I believe You died for my sin and only through faith in Your death and resurrection can I be forgiven. I want to turn from my sin and ask You to come into my life as my Savior and Lord. From this day on, I will follow You by living a life that pleases You. Thank You, Lord Jesus, for loving and forgiving me. Amen."

After you have asked Jesus Christ into your life, tell a Christian friend and follow Christ in believer's baptism and church membership. You'll find there are others who will love and support you.

This booklet can be a great tool to use for a group study. You may study it with a Sunday School class, in a home Bible study, on a retreat, or in a Christian club on your school campus.

You can find suggestions for leading a group study based on this booklet at:

www.truelovewaits.com

A LifeWay Ministry

True Love Waits Commitment

Believing that true love waits, I make a commitment to God, myself, my family, my friends, my future mate, and my future children to a lifetime of purity including sexual abstinence from this day until the day I enter a biblical marriage relationship.

Signature _____

Date _____